Christal Lorice Bailey is a former elementary and middle school teacher. She enjoys writing poetry, gardening, singing karaoke, listening to a variety of music genres, and dancing. Her passions are children's literacy, animal welfare, and global travel. She served in the Air Force and is a graduate of the University of Utah and Lesley University.

Christal Lorice Bailey

ANIMALIA
A to Z

AUSTIN MACAULEY PUBLISHERS®

LONDON * CAMBRIDGE * NEW YORK * SHARJAH

Ordering Information
Quantity sales: Special discounts are available on quantity purchases by corporations, associations, and others. For details, contact the publisher at the address below.

Publisher's Cataloging-in-Publication data
Bailey, Christal Lorice
Animalia: A to Z

ISBN 9798891554900 (Paperback)
ISBN 9798891554917 (e-Pub e-book)

Library of Congress Control Number: 2024915196

www.austinmacauley.com/us

First Published 2024
Austin Macauley Publishers LLC
40 Wall Street, 33rd Floor, Suite 3302
New York, NY 10005
USA

mail-usa@austinmacauley.com
+1 (646) 5125767

For my granddaughter, Emma G. Thanks for helping me
to love teaching and learning again.

Thank you to Jasmine Stewart, Louis Bailey, and Thameera
Rohan for your support and contributions to this book.

Dear Young Scientist,

Biologists categorize living things on Earth into six kingdoms:

1. Archaebacteria
2. Eubacteria
3. Protista
4. Plantae
5. Fungi
6. Animalia (the most complex organism)

This book's focus is on Animalia only. The other kingdoms are very interesting, too. As you move up in grade levels, you will learn more about the other kingdoms.

Happy reading!

Aa
Axolotl: Amphibian

Habitat: Primarily found in the lakes and ponds of Mexico (North America).

Diet: Small fish, worms, and larvae.

Life span: 5 to 6 years in the wild.

Average adult weight: 8 ounces (227 grams).

Young axolotls are called larvae.

A group of axolotls is called a harem or clutch.

Predators: Storks and herons.

They are primarily at risk because of pollution in the waters where they live.

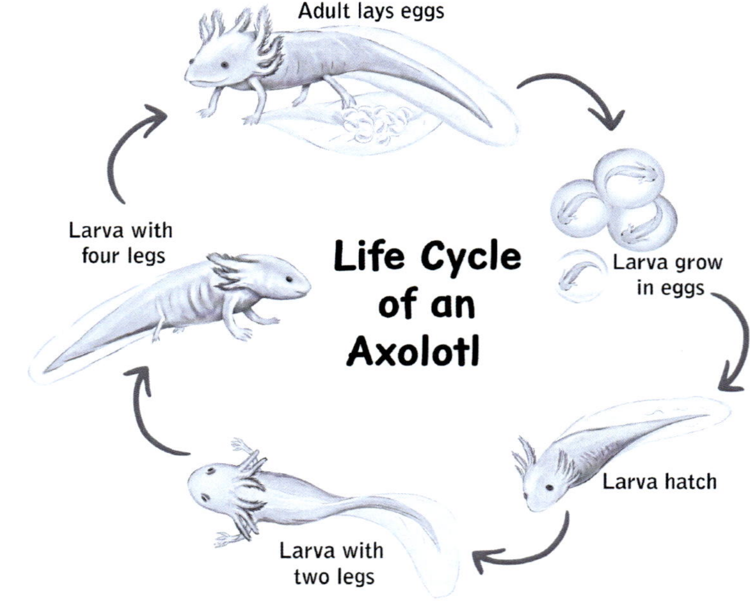

Its name comes from the ancient Aztec language of Nahuatl. The name "axolotl" is loosely translated to "water dog." Axolotls are critically endangered, which means they could be extinct within 10 to 20 years without human intervention. The axolotl has the ability to regenerate/regrow lost limbs. They are usually dark in color and camouflage themselves by making their skin lighter or darker as needed. The pink varieties are bred by humans to make them look cuter. Regardless of their color, they are delightful!

Bb

Badger: Mammal

Habitat: A variety of this species is found around the world; however, the species depicted here is found in the grasslands and deserts of North America.

Diet: Snakes, lizards, frogs, mice, bird eggs, and insects.

Life span: 9 to 15 years in the wild.

Average adult weight: 10 to 24 pounds (approximately 5 to 11 kilograms).

Young badgers are called cubs.

A group of badgers is called a cete.

Predators: Eagles, bears, wolves, and cougars.

The badger is a member of the weasel family and is related to polecats, wolverines, skunks, and ferrets. They live and hunt where the soil is soft enough for them to dig for their food. They have poor vision, but their senses of hearing and smelling are strong. Unfortunately, badgers are hunted for their pelts and are often hit by cars. Don't even think about keeping a badger as a pet! Badgers are aggressive and extremely unlikely to be domesticated. There are many species of badgers. The badger depicted here is an American badger, and you can find it in Eastern Washington State.

Cc

Clouded Leopard: Mammal

Habitat: The tropical forests of Southeast Asia.

Diet: Monkeys, wild pigs, birds, and deer.

Life span: 12 to 15 years.

Average adult weight: Males – 40 to 50 pounds (18.1 to 22.7 kilograms); females – 25 to 30 pounds (11.3 to 13.6 kilograms).

Young clouded leopards are called cubs.

A group of leopards is called a leap.

Predators: Tigers.

The greatest threats to the clouded leopard are human beings.

The leopards' pelts are in demand around the world.

The cubs stay with their mothers for 9 to 10 months while learning to hunt and survive on their own. A cub is usually born with two siblings. The leopards rest in the trees and spend time hunting on the ground. Compared to other big cats, the clouded leopard has the longest canine teeth. They are great climbers and have a very long tail that helps them maintain balance. As of July 2024, you can visit the Asian Forest Sanctuary at Point Defiance Zoo to see a real clouded leopard!

Dd

Darkling Beetle: Insect

Habitat: Worldwide (mostly in dry, warm climates).
Diet: Dead insects and decaying vegetation.
Life span: 3 to 15 years.
Average weight: Less than an ounce (130 to 160 milligrams).
Young darkling beetles are called larva.
A group of beetles is called a swarm.
Predators: Snakes, hawks, and coyotes.

There are over 1,200 species of this beetle in Canada, the United States, and Mexico. The darkling beetle doesn't bite but releases a stinky smell to defend itself. They get most of their hydration (water) from the foods they eat. The female beetle can lay 2,000 eggs per year. Some darkling beetles have wings and can fly, while others move around by walking. Many farmers consider them pests because they snack on their crops, but these beetles are harmless to humans.

Ee

Emperor Penguin: Bird

Habitat: The tundra of Antarctica.
Diet: Fish, krill, and squid.
Life span: 15 to 20 years in the wild.
Average adult weight: For males and females – 45 to 50 pounds
(18.1 to 22.7 kilograms).
Young emperor penguins are called chicks.
A group of penguins on land is called a waddle.
In the water, they are called a raft.
Predators: Orcas and leopard seals.

They are the largest in the penguin species. The female lays a single egg in June and then departs for the ocean to eat. The male stays behind and cares for the egg until it hatches in August. The female returns in August to take care of the chick. and the male returns to the ocean to eat. He has lost a lot of weight. having not eaten for months. Emperor penguins live in extremely cold temperatures, -58° Celsius or -50° Fahrenheit. Life in Antarctica is harsh, isn't it?

Ff

Fainting Goat:

Habitat: Tennessee / USA / North America.
Diet: Hay, grains, grasses, salt, and mineral blocks.
Life span: 12 to 15 years.
Average adult weight: Males – 80 to 175 pounds (36.3 to
79.4 kilograms); females – 50 to 110 pounds
(23.7 to 59.0 kilograms).
Young female goats are called "does" and young male goats
are called "bucks."
A group of goats is called a herd.
Predators: Coyotes, bears, cougars, and other large animals.

The myotonic or Tennessee fainting goat does not actually faint. Its muscles stiffen or contract when surprised by unexpected sounds or when it is overly excited. It does appear that the goat experiences any pain when this happens. Younger goats tend to fall over. while older goats may simply stiffen. It takes a minute or two for it to recover and stand. Then, it's back to prancing around! These stocky animals are good-natured and make good pets. If you want a small, easy-to-care-for farm animal, the fainting goat is a great choice.

Gg

Glass Frog: Amphibian

Habitat: The humid forests of Central and South America.

Diet: Crickets, spiders, moths, and flies

Life span: 10 to 14 years.

Average weight: 0.2 to 0.5 ounces (5 to 14 grams).

Young frogs are called tadpoles.

A group of frogs is called a colony.

Predators: Snakes, small mammals, and birds.

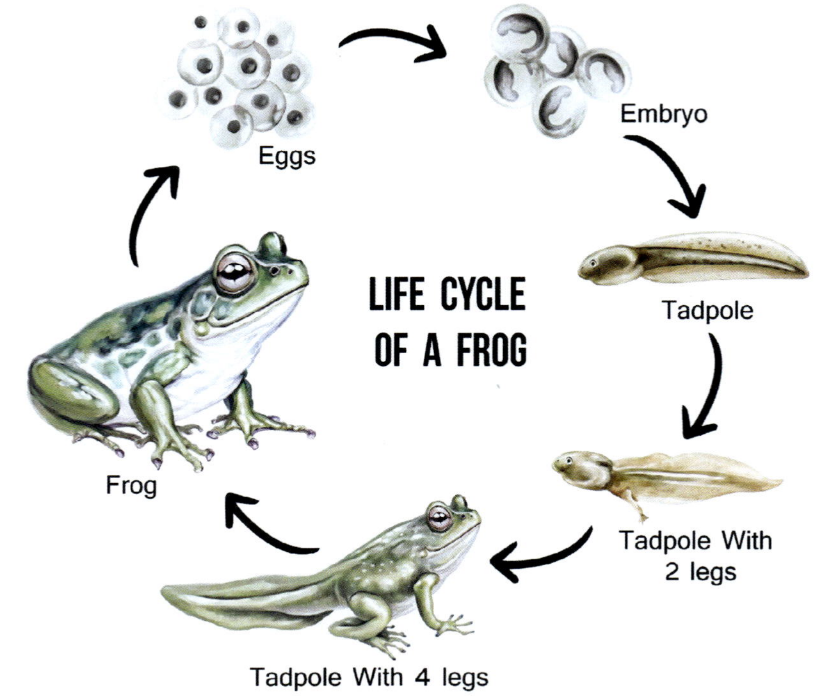

Glass frogs are arboreal, which means they live in trees but spend time looking for food near water. Some glass frogs are translucent; when you look at their belly and chest areas, you can see their internal organs, bones, and beating heart! They can jump large distances to escape being a predator's dinner. Many species of glass frogs are either vulnerable or endangered. They require a special habitat, so they do not make good pets unless you are able to keep up with the cost of maintaining it.

Hh

Hawksbill Turtle: Reptile

Habitat: The remote beaches of the Atlantic/Caribbean and Indian Oceans.
Diet: Sea sponges, algae, mollusks, and small fish.
Life span: 50 to 60 years.
Average adult weight: 100 to 150 pounds (45.4 to 68.0 kilograms).
Young Hawksbill turtles are called hatchlings.
A group of turtles is called a bale.
Predators: Sharks, octopi, and crocodiles.

Hawksbill turtles spend most of their time in the water. The female comes to the shore to lay her clutch of 120 to 140 eggs. The eggs hatch as a group and return to the sea a few weeks later. Adult turtles help keep coral reefs free from sea sponges, which can weaken the coral's structure. These turtles are a critically endangered species because they are hunted for their beautiful shells. Unfortunately, humans also take their eggs. Many turtles are trapped in fishing nets and are injured or killed.

Ii

Ibis: Bird

Habitat: Swamps, marshlands, and wetlands around the world.
Diet: Fish, crabs, grasshoppers, crayfish, snakes, frogs, and insects.
Life span: 15 to 20 years in the wild.
Average adult weight: 2 to 3 pounds (0.91 to 1.37 kilograms).
Young ibises are called chicks.
A group of ibises is called a stand or congregation on land and a flock or wedge when flying.
Predators: Falcons, hawks, and herons.

There are many species of ibises, but the one pictured here is the White Ibis. It is found throughout Florida. The ibis has a long, curved bill for digging in muddy surfaces for food. It has a wingspan of 3 feet (about 96 centimeters). The male is very protective of the nest; however, both ibis parents take care of and feed the chicks. Ibises are very social birds as they live and travel in flocks. If you visit Florida, be sure to look up. You may see these beautiful birds flying in a V-formation.

Jj

Jerboa: Mammal

Habitat: The deserts of North Africa and Asia.

Diet: Seeds, plants, and insects.

Life span: 4 to 6 years in the wild.

Average adult weight: 2 to 3 ounces (0.057 to 0.085 kilograms).

Young jerboas are called pups.

A group of jerboas has no collective name; read the explanation below.

Predators: Owls, cats, foxes, and snakes.

The jerboa, because it lives in desert climates, sleeps during the day and forages for food at night to stay cool. It does not drink water but obtains liquid from the food it eats. Thanks to its big ears, the jerboa can use the sense of hearing to track its prey. Jerboas are adorable and hop like a kangaroo! Jerboas are great diggers and prefer to live alone in individual burrows or underground homes. If you love animals, you would not have a jerboa as a pet because it would not thrive in captivity.

Kk

Komodo Dragon: Reptile

Habitat: The Indonesian Islands.
Diet: Pigs, deer, water buffalo, and carcasses.
Life span: 25 to 35 years in the wild.
Average adult weight: 150 t0 300 pounds (68 to 136 kilograms).
Young komodo dragons are called pups or hatchlings.
A group of Komodo dragons is called a bank.
Predators: In its native habitat, Komodo dragons have no natural predators.

The Komodo dragon, also known as the Komodo monitor, is the largest and heaviest lizard on earth. It is slow-moving but has powerful claws and legs. It also has a forked tongue that it uses to taste the air. Komodos are fierce hunters. If the prey manages to escape after being bitten by the Komodo's sharp, jagged teeth, it won't live for long. The Komodo Dragon's saliva is filled with bacteria that will kill its meal within hours. All the Komodo has to do is track the smell to find its meal.

Ll

Lyrebird: Bird

Habitat: The bushland and rainforests of Australia (Oceania).

Diet: Insects, worms, spiders, and seeds.

Life span: 25 to 30 years.

Average adult weight: 2 to 3 pounds. Baby lyrebirds are called chicks.

A group of lyrebirds is called a musket.

Predators: Other birds of prey, habitat destruction, hunting for is feathers, quolls, and feral cats.

The lyrebird doesn't move around a lot; it prefers to stay within a small area. It spends most of its time on the ground but will roost in trees. It isn't the best in flight either, but will fly if it feels threatened. When a male lyrebird wants to mate, it sings and dances for the female's attention. It can mimic the calls of other birds. There are two types of this bird, the Superb Lyrebird, and Albert's Lyrebird.

Mm

Malabar Giant Squirrel: Mammal/ Rodent

Habitat: The tropical forests and woodlands of India (Eurasia).
Diet: Fruits, flowers, nuts, insects, and bird eggs.
Life span: 15 to 20 years.
Average adult weight: 4 to 6 pounds (about 2 to 3 kilograms).
Young Malabar giant squirrels are called kits or kittens.
A group of squirrels is called a scurry.
Predators: Leopards and birds of prey.

The Malabar giant squirrel, also known as the Indian Giant Squirrel, is arboreal. It is native to India, which means it is not found anywhere else in the world. They can jump great distances from tree to tree. They are very friendly and can be fed by humans. Although they are not in the vulnerable, threatened, or endangered classification, they are losing their habitat to the construction of dams and the deforestation.

Nn

Narwhal: Mammal

Habitat: Arctic waters of Canada, Greenland (North America),
Russia, Finland (Eurasia).
Diet: Cod, squid, halibut, and shrimp.
Life span: 40 to 50 years.
Average adult weight: Males – 3,200 pounds (1,452 kilograms);
females – 2,200 pounds (998 kilograms).
Young narwhals are called calves.
A group of narwhals is called a blessing.
Predators: Killer whales and polar bears.

Narwhals are well-suited for living in or near the Arctic because they have thick blubber that covers most of their body. Narwhals live and travel in groups of up to twenty. During the summer, thousands of them can be seen swimming and playing together. They are deep divers and can hold their breath for as long as 25 minutes! Can you see why narwhals have the nickname of "sea unicorn?" Unfortunately, poachers hunt them for their ivory tusks.

Oo

Owl Butterfly: Insect

Habitat: The rainforests of Central and South America, Mexico.
Diet: The juice of rotting fruit and pollen.
Life span: About 18 weeks.
Average weight: Less than 1 ounce.
A group of butterflies is called a kaleidoscope.
Predators: Birds and lizards.

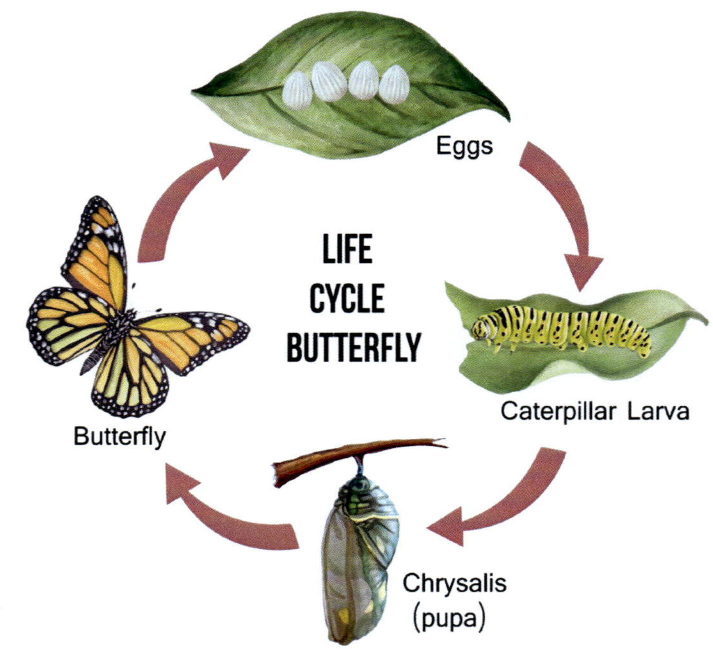

Owl butterflies cannot eat solid food; they must turn their food into a liquid before digesting it. The liquid makes the butterflies a bit tipsy because of fermentation or the turning of the juice into alcohol. The spots on their wings resemble the eyes of an owl, which provides protection from predators. It is one of the largest butterflies in South America with a wingspan of 8 inches or about 20 centimeters. Because of their large size, they cannot fly great distances. To stay safe, the owl butterfly is active mostly at night where they are not easily seen. The natural coloring also allows this butterfly to camouflage itself against the tree bark.

Pp

Potoo: Bird

Habitat: The rainforests of Central and South America.
Diet: Grasshoppers, termites, and beetles.
Life span: Undocumented but believed to be between 12 to
14 years.
Average adult weight: 12 to 22 ounces (340–624 grams).
Young potoos are called a chicks.
A group of potoos is called a flock.
Predators: Monkeys and falcons.

The great potoo has enormous googly eyes and a wide mouth. The eyes help the potoo hunt at night, and they can be from brown to yellow in color. A big mouth helps it capture a large amount of flying insects. The feathers blend into the natural surroundings for safety and protection. It lets out a haunting cry like a short, gravelly growl, so it can sound like an angry ghost. Imagine hearing that at night in the forest!

Qq

Quetzal: Bird

Habitat: The mountainous rainforests of Central America
and South America.
Diet: Fruits, insects, and berries.
Life span: 5 to 10 years.
Average weight: 8 ounces (0.20 kilograms).
Young quetzals are called nestlings.
A group of quetzals is called a flock.
Predators: Owls, squirrels, and hawks.

The biggest threat to this beautiful bird is deforestation, which is the cutting down of trees. They are not the best fliers and prefer to perch in trees. There are many varieties of quetzals, but the one depicted here is the resplendent quetzal. Isn't it beautiful? Fun fact: the quetzal is the currency (money) of Guatemala, a country in Central America.

Rr

Red Panda: Mammal

Habitat: The mountainous range Burma, Nepal, India, China, Myanmar, and Bhutan (Eurasia).
Diet: Mainly bamboo, but will eat fruit and insects.
Life span: 7 to 8 years in the wild; up to 14 years in zoos.
Average weight: Depending on the species and gender, 6 to 14 pounds (3 to 6 kilograms).
Young red pandas are called cubs.
A group of red pandas is called a pack.
Predators: Snow leopards.

As of 2024, the ICUN* lists red pandas as endangered. According to the same agency, there are less than 10,000 worldwide. The biggest threat to these adorable animals is the loss of their habitat and climate change. There are two species of the red panda, with one slightly larger than the other. They are solitary creatures and spend the hottest part of the day sleeping. They are sometimes called the "lesser panda," but they are just as important to biodiversity as the giant panda. As of July 2024, you can visit a red panda at Seattle's Woodland Park Zoo.

Ss

Sloth: Mammal

Habitat: Tropical rainforests of Central and South America.
Diet: Mainly leaves, but will eat fruit.
Life Span: 20 to 25 years.
Average adult weight: Between 8 and 17 pounds (3.6 to 7.7 kilograms).
Young sloths are called babies.
A group of sloths has no official name, although the Sloth Conservation Foundation held an online naming contest, and the winning name was "snuggle." A snuggle of sloths. What do you think of the name?
Predators: Jaguars, ocelots, harpy eagles, and hawks.

Sloths are arboreal, nocturnal, and sleep 15 to 18 hours per day. There are two groups of sloth types: two-fingered and three-fingered. Sloths are related to armadillos and anteaters. They spend a lot of time hanging upside down in trees and only come down to poop! They are great swimmers but move very slowly when on the ground. Actually, they are the slowest mammal in the world. The greatest risk to their survival is deforestation.

Tt

Tangerine Leopard Gecko: Reptile

Habitat: Deserts of Nepal, Afghanistan, Pakistan, and India (Eurasia).
Diet: Mealworms and crickets.
Life span: 10 to 20 years in captivity.
Average adult size: 7 to 11 inches long (18 to 28 cm); 2 to 2.5 ounces (50 to 70 grams).
A group of geckos is called a hype.
Predators: Foxes, owls, snakes, and larger lizards in the wild.

This gecko can come with different shades of tangerine. The color may be all over its body or just on the head or tail. Please purchase your gecko from a reputable dealer. If you decide to get this colorful little creature as a pet, make sure you provide it with the proper indoor habitat. It needs a ten-gallon enclosure with a lid, a heat lamp, and a safe material to line the bottom of the tank. Remember, they can live a long time, so be prepared to be a pet parent for quite a while.

Uu

Uakari: Mammal

*(pronounced wuh-**kaa**-ree)*
Habitat: The tropical forests of Brazil, Peru, and Columbia
(South America).
Diet: Fruit, leaves, and insects.
Life span: 15 to 30 years.
Average weight: 7 pounds or 3.2 kilograms.
Young uakaris are called infants.
A group of uakaris is called a troop.
Predators: Humans hunt them for food.

Deforestation is also a threat to their habitat.
The name may begin with the letter "u," but it is actually pronounced with a "w" sound. They are intelligent and playful primates. The redder its face, the better looking it is to attract a mate. Ask a parent or guardian to help you research why this animal has a bright, red face. According to the IUCN, uakaris are "vulnerable" in the wild.

Vv

Vampire Bat: Mammal

Habitat: Caves, mines, abandoned buildings in North America, Central America, and South America.
Diet: Blood.
Life span: 8 to 12 years.
Average adult weight: 2 ounces (0.06 kilograms).
Young vampire bats are called pups.
A group of bats is called a colony.
Predators: Eagles and hawks.

Bats don't have the best reputation thanks to scary movies and Halloween. However, they are not likely to feed on the blood of humans. They do not suck blood. Rather, they bite their victim, and as the blood flows, they lap it up like a cat laps up water. The saliva of the bat leaves a substance in and around the wound that keeps the blood from clotting or stopping. Bats rarely kill their prey. A bat is the only mammal to feed only on blood and fly.

Ww

Wombat: Mammal/Marsupial

Habitat: Forests, grasslands, and shrublands of Australia.
Diet: Grasses.
Life span: 18 to 24 years.
Average adult weight: 44 to 77 (20 to 35 kilograms).
Young wombats are called joeys.
A group of wombats is called a wisdom.
Predators: Eagles, foxes, dingoes, and Tasmanian Devils.

Wombats like to be alone. During the day, they sleep up to 16 hours in a burrow. At night, they look for food. Because of the climate of Australia, wombats can tolerate very warm temperatures and can survive long periods of time without water. Wombats have cube-shaped poop! After pooping, they scatter the pieces around their territory to warn other wombats to stay away. Wombats are cute and cuddly but do not make good pets. If you see one in the wild, do not attempt to pet it or you might get clawed and bitten.

Xx

Xoloitzcuintli: Mammal

*(pronounced show-low-etz-**queent**-lee)*
Habitat: They are pets in homes around the world.
Diet: High-quality dog food and fresh water.
Lifespan: 10 to 12 years.
Average weight: 30 to 55 pounds (13.7 to 25 kilograms).
Young Xolos are called puppies.
A group of Xolos is called a pack.
Predators: None.

The original hairless dog was bred in Mexico. According to the American Kennel Association (AKC), Xolos are bred in two varieties, hairless and coated. They are playful, easy-going, and enjoy long walks. The breed is rare and very expensive. Provided with appropriate veterinary care, the Xolo will be a lifelong friend.

Yy

Yak: Mammal

Habitat: The grassland of the Himalayan Mountains (Eurasia).

Diet: Grass, herbs, and wildflowers.

Life span: 20 to 25 years in human care.

Average adult weight: 900 to 1,200 pounds (approximately 408 to 544 kilograms).

Young yaks are called calves.

A group of yaks is called a herd.

Predators: Tibetan wolves and snow leopards.

There are two types of yaks.

1) Tibetan yaks are domesticated and help traders and farmers transport goods and food. Because they have large lungs, they are well-adapted to breathe the thin air at higher elevations. Yak mothers are protective of their babies but are not usually a threat to humans. A yak's milk can be made into butter and cheese. Yaks are quite agile considering their size; they can climb steep mountains and slippery rocks with ease.

2) The wild yak is an endangered breed due to poaching and loss of habitat. It is believed that there are less than 10,000 yaks living in the wild.

Zz

Zebu: Mammal

Habitat: Tropical rainforest, jungles, wetlands of South Eurasia
and Africa.
Diet: Leaves, grasses, and shrubs.
Life span: 15 to 20 years.
Average adult weight: 1,000 pounds (454 kilograms).
Young zebus are called calves.
A group of zebus is called a herd.
Predators: Tigers, crocodiles, and wolves.

The zebu belongs to the bovine family, which includes cows, cattle, bison, and buffalo. They tolerate hot, dry climates. They are generally used for heavy work such as pulling carts. There are many species of zebus, and most are in India and Africa. Like a camel, the zebu has a hump. The hump on the zebu may be there for fat and water storage like the camel, but unlike the camel's hump, there is muscle in and bone under the zebu's hump. Fun fact: Zebus have four sections in their stomachs, while we humans only have one.

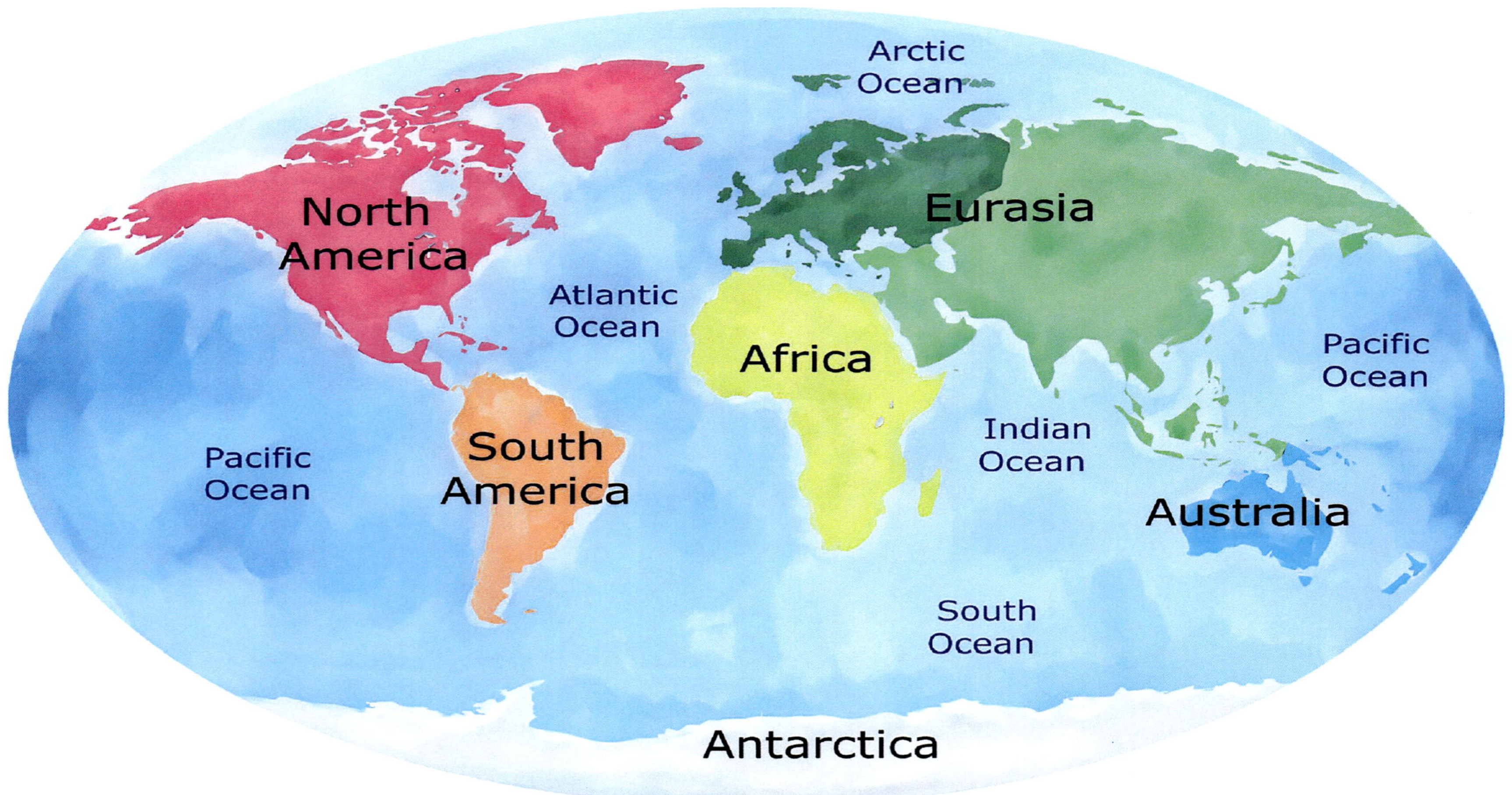

Arctic
Ocean
North
America
Eurasia
Atlantic
Ocean
Africa
Pacific
Ocean
Pacific
Ocean
South
America
Indian
Ocean
Australia
South
Ocean
Antarctica

Glossary

The Kingdom of Animalia (Simple Version)

Amphibians – Vertebrate animals that can live in water and on land.
Birds – Vertebrate animals that have feathers and fly (not all birds can fly).
Aquatic – Vertebrate and invertebrate animals found in the freshwater and saltwater.
Insects – An animal with a segmented body and an exoskeleton.
Mammals – Vertebrate animals that typically have live births, hair or fur, and females produce milk for their young.
Marsupial – A type of mammal that can have a pouch to nurture its young.
Rodent – A type of mammal that has the need to chew due to their constantly growing front teeth (incisors).
Reptiles – Vertebrate animals that are cold-blooded and have a scaly body.

- Agile – Able to move quickly and easily.
- Arboreal – Living in or among trees.
- Aquatic – Living in or growing in water.
- Aztec – An ancient civilization that existed in what is now present-day Mexico.
- Burrow – A hole or tunnel in the ground made by an animal for shelter and safety.
- Camouflage – An animal's way of hiding itself from predators.
- Carcass – The body of a dead animal.
- Carnivore – Any mammal that eats meat and/or fish as its primary source of food.
- Climate – The overall weather conditions of a particular region of the earth.
- Cold-blooded – Ay animal whose blood temperature changes due to its surrounding area.
- Deforestation – The clearing of a forest or wooded area, leaving few or no trees.
- Diurnal – Active during the day and rests at night.
- Domesticated – Tamed to live and work among humans.

- Exoskeleton – The hard structure outside of a body used for protection, such as a shell.
- Forage – To search for food.
- Herbivore – Any animal which eats plants as its primary source of food.
- Nocturnal – Active at night.
- Omnivore – Any animal that eats meat, fish, and plants.
- Pelt – The skin and fur of an animal.
- Predator – Any animal that hunts and eats other animals.
- Prey – Any animal that is hunted for food.
- Rainforest – An area of tall trees that receives a high amount of rainfall.
- Rodent – Animals that have a continuously growing pair of front teeth (incisors).
- Roost – A place for birds to rest at night.
- Tundra – A very cold habitat that receives very little rainfall or snowfall.
- Vertebrate – Any animal with a backbone or spine.

* The International Union for the Conservation of Nature (IUCN)™ is the world's most comprehensive information source on the global extinction risk status of animal, fungus, and plant species. Open to all, it is used by governmental bodies, non-profit organizations, businesses, and individuals.

Red List Categories:

- Least concern – Currently, there is no threat to its survival.
- Vulnerable – A weakened ability to recover from human-made or natural disasters.
- Near Threatened – Likely to become endangered in the near future.
- Endangered – High risk of extinction in the wild.
- Critically Endangered – Extremely high risk of extinction in the wild.
- Extinct in the Wild – The species is only found in zoos or sanctuaries.
- Extinct – No member of the species exists.
- Data Deficient – Not enough information to determine status.
- Not Evaluated.

https://www.iucn.org/resources/conservation-tool/iucn-red-list-threatened-species
Accessed June 21, 2023, at 5:40 pm.

For Educators and Parents

Second Grade Common Core State Standards for Reading Informational Text

Craft and Structure:

- Know and use the various text features (e.g., captions, bolded print, subheadings, glossaries, indexes) to locate key facts or information in a text efficiently.
- Identify the main purpose of a text, including what the author wants to answer, explain, or describe.

Integration of Knowledge and Ideas:

- Explain how specific images contribute to and clarify a text.
- Range of Reading and Level of Text Complexity.
- By the end of the year, read and comprehend informational text (including history/social studies, science) in the grades 2–3 complexity band proficiently, with scaffolding at the high end of the range.

https://learning.ccsso.org/wp-content/uploads/2022/11/ADA-Compliant-ELA-Standards.pdf

Second Grade DCI Arrangements of the Next Generation Science Standards

Biological Evolution and Unity Diversity:

Make observations of plants and animals to compare the diversity of life in different habitats. [Clarification Statement: Emphasis is on the diversity of living things in each of a variety of different habitats.]

- There are many different kinds of living things in any area, and they exist in different places on land and in water.

https://www.k12.wa.us/sites/default/files/public/science/pubdocs/DCI%20Arrangements%20of%20the%20Next%20Generation%20Science%20Standards.pdf

National Council for Geography Standards

Essential Element 1: The World in Spatial Terms

- Standard 1: How to use maps and other geographic representations, tools, and technologies to acquire, process, and report information from a spatial perspective.
- Standard 2: How to use mental maps to organize information about people, places, and environments in a spatial context.
- Standard 3: How to analyze the spatial organization of people, places, and environments on Earth's surface.

https://ncge.org/teacher-resources/national-geography-standards/

Common Core State Standards for Second Grade Mathematics

A.   Measure and estimate lengths in standard units.

- Measure the length of an object by selecting and using appropriate tools such as rulers, yardsticks, meter sticks, and measuring tapes.
- Measure the length of an object twice, using length units of different lengths for the two measurements; describe how the two measurements relate to the size of the unit chosen.
- Estimate lengths using units of inches, feet, centimeters, and meters.
- Measure to determine how much longer one object is than another, expressing the length difference in terms of a standard length unit.

https://learning.ccsso.org/wp-content/uploads/2022/11/ADA-Compliant-Math-Standards.pdf

Standard to Metric Conversions for Weight

1 ounce = approximately 28 grams (g)

16 ounces =1 pound = approximately 454 grams (g)

Standard to Metric Conversions for Length

1 inch = 2.54 centimeters (cm)

12 inches = 1 foot = 30.48 centimeters (cm)

3 feet= 1 yard = 91.44 centimeters (cm)

Common Core State Standards for Second Grade Writing

- Write opinion pieces in which they introduce the topic or book they are writing about, state an opinion, supply reasons that support the opinion, use linking words (e.g., because, and, also) to connect opinion and reasons, and provide a concluding statement or section.
- Write informative/explanatory texts in which they introduce a topic, use facts and definitions to develop points, and provide a concluding statement or section.

https://learning.ccsso.org/wp-content/uploads/2022/11/ADA-Compliant-ELA-Standards.pdf

Learn more about Animalia by checking out these websites for children:

https://animalfactguide.com

https://kids.nationalgeographic.com/animals

https://switchzoo.com/

https://www.zooborns.com/

https://www.wwf.org.uk/

https://www.worldwildlife.org/species

https://a-z-animals.com/animals/location/north-america/united-states/washington/

Careers working in the kingdom of Animalia:

Animal Breede	Animal Control Officer	Animal Trainer
Animal Welfare	Biologist	Conservation Officer
Dog Groomer	Dog Walker	Entomologist
Farrier	Kennel Attendant	Lab Animal Technician
Marine Biologist	Pet Sitter	Ranch Manager
Veterinarian	Veterinary Technician	Wildlife Biologist
Wildlife Photographer	Wildlife Rehabilitation	Zookeeper
Zoologist		

About the author:

Christal is a former public school teacher and Air Force veteran. She enjoys reading, writing poems, gardening, and traveling. She is the pet parent of a rescued terrier mix named Cosette and a rescued cat named LilyBelle. Christal lives in beautiful Tacoma, WA.

About the illustrator:

Thameera is a digital graphic artist and wedding photographer. He lives in Ambalangoda, Galle, Sri Lanka.